OVERTURNED

The Constitutional Right to Abortion

Carla Mooney

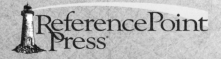

ReferencePoint
Press®

San Diego, CA

About the Author

Carla Mooney is the author of many books for young adults and children. She lives in Pittsburgh, Pennsylvania, with her husband and three children.

Picture Credits:
Cover: Shutterstock

7: Heidi Besen/Alamy Stock Photo
13: MediaPunch Inc/Alamy Stock Photo
16: PixelPro/Alamy Stock Photo
20: Fred Schilling Collection, Collection of the
   Supreme Court of the United States
28: Maury Aaseng
30: Reuters/Alamy Stock Photo

33: Associated Press
37: Gorodenkoff/Shutterstock
39: nensuria/iStock
44: Reuters/Alamy Stock Photo
46: turtix/Shutterstock
49: Associated Press
52: Reuters/Alamy Stock Image
54: Zuma Press/Alamy Stock Image
56: Cavan Images/Alamy Stock Photo

LIBRARY OF CONGRESS CATALOGING-IN-PUBLICATION DATA

Names: Mooney, Carla, 1970- author.
Title: Overturned : the constitutional right to abortion / by Carla Mooney.
Description: San Diego : ReferencePoint Press, 2023. | Includes
   bibliographical references and index.
Identifiers: LCCN 2022043892 (print) | LCCN 2022043893 (ebook) | ISBN
   9781678205126 (library binding) | ISBN 9781678205133 (ebook)
Subjects: LCSH: Abortion--Law and legislation--United States--Juvenile
   literature. | Abortion--Moral and ethical aspects--United
   States--Juvenile literature. | Roe, Jane, 1947-2017--Trials, litigation,
   etc.--Juvenile literature. | Wade, Henry--Trials, litigation,
   etc.--Juvenile literature. | Trials (Abortion)--Washington
   (D.C.)--Juvenile literature.
Classification: LCC KF3771 .M66 2022 (print) | LCC KF3771 (ebook) | DDC
   342.7308/4--dc23/eng/20220930
LC record available at https://lccn.loc.gov/2022043892
LC ebook record available at https://lccn.loc.gov/2022043893

CONTENTS

The Ruling That Shook a Nation

On June 24, 2022, the US Supreme Court issued a monumental decision to overturn *Roe v. Wade*, the 1973 landmark ruling that established the constitutional right to abortion in the United States. By a vote of 5–4, the court ruled that the US Constitution does not guarantee the right to obtain an abortion. This decision does not make abortion illegal. Rather, it directs lawmakers in each state to decide whether to allow abortion in their state and what, if any, restrictions to place on the procedure if it remains legal.

Swift Reaction: Grief and Rage

Reactions to the court's decision came quickly from people on both sides of the abortion issue. Abortion rights supporters condemned the ruling. Thousands gathered in Washington, DC, and other cities to protest the court's reversal of *Roe*. Although a leaked draft opinion previewed the court's decision in May, many protesters were still shocked that the court had reversed the decades-old ruling.

In New York City thousands of abortion rights supporters gathered in Union Square, marched downtown, and chanted, "Abortion is health care, health care is a right."[1] Sixteen-year-old Anura Bracey was one of the protesters who joined the march. Like many other protesters, she felt rage and grief over the court's decision. "I'm enraged. I'm terrified for what this means for birthing people in the country," she says. "I want someone to listen to us. I don't know how much this is really going to do, but I just feel very desperate."[2]

A few hours after the ruling's release, US attorney general Merrick Garland issued a statement strongly disagreeing with the court's decision to overturn *Roe v. Wade*. "This decision deals a devastating blow to reproductive freedom in the United States. It will have an immediate and irreversible impact on the lives of people across the country," he said. Garland also promised that the US Department of Justice would work to protect reproductive freedom for all Americans. He said:

> The ability to decide one's own future is a fundamental American value, and few decisions are more significant and personal than the choice of whether and when to have children. Few rights are more central to individual freedom than the right to control one's own body. The Justice Department will use every tool at our disposal to protect reproductive freedom. And we will not waver from this Department's founding responsibility to protect the civil rights of all Americans.[3]

Celebrations in the Streets

While abortion rights supporters protested, antiabortion activists gathered at locations across the nation to celebrate the court's decision. Many had worked for decades to overturn the constitutional right to abortion. Abortion opponents nationwide were overjoyed by the court's ruling, an outcome many believed would never occur in their lifetime.

After the ruling, antiabortion activist Lauren Handy celebrated with other like-minded people in Washington, DC. She described her feelings upon hearing the news: "It's a roller-coaster of emotion. Complete and utter joy it was finally overturned." Her work is not done, however. She says abortion opponents will work toward outlawing abortion in liberal (or blue) states that have vowed to protect abortion rights. "The abortion industrial complex is strong in blue states, and we gotta go after them as well,"[4] she says.

Outside the Supreme Court, Penny Nance, president of Concerned Women for America, a nonprofit conservative legislative action committee, gathered with other abortion opponents to pray. Nance firmly believes that life begins at conception. She argues that modern medical advancements prove that a fetus is a human being with the right to life. As news of the court's ruling spread, Nance celebrated. "Today, a grievous wrong was righted. In 1973, seven men decided for the entire country. They halted a conversation that was going. Science caught up with the lie of abortion," she says. "I feel such incredible and deep gratitude, first to God, that I got to live to see this moment."[5]

> "Today, a grievous wrong was righted. In 1973, seven men decided for the entire country. They halted a conversation that was going. Science caught up with the lie of abortion."[5]
>
> —Penny Nance, president of Concerned Women for America

Impact of the Ruling

The court's ruling gives individual states the power to determine their abortion laws and restrictions. In creating their laws, states are no longer restricted by *Roe*, which disallowed any effort to impede a woman's ability to obtain an abortion during the first two trimesters of pregnancy.

Nearly half of US states are expected to outlaw or significantly restrict abortion. This process has already begun. As of late August 2022, twelve states had banned most abortions. Some states have been expanding their restrictions in an effort to prevent women from traveling to other states for the procedure or from obtaining information about abortions from anyone, including their health care providers. These laws, if allowed to stand, would impact millions of women in the United States. Experts note that abortion will still be available to women who can afford

Abortion rights supporters march in protest of the Supreme Court's ruling that overturned Roe v. Wade.

to travel to states where it is legal. Those who do not have the means to do that may be faced with the choice of an unsafe illegal abortion or carrying an unwanted child.

New Challenges Ahead

The 1973 *Roe* decision did not end the abortion debate in the United States. Rather, it prompted many legal challenges. The new ruling is expected to have a similar effect. Lawsuits have already been filed in many states and are likely to continue as lawmakers in those states tighten restrictions on how women obtain reproductive health care. The ruling has set in motion an immense shift in public health policies affecting pregnant women and families.

This is happening despite the ruling being unpopular with a majority of Americans. Surveys have consistently shown that most Americans believe that *Roe* should remain in effect and abortion, with some restrictions, should be legal. An NPR/*PBS NewsHour*/Marist poll conducted immediately after the court's decision was made public revealed no change in these views. In that poll, 56 percent of respondents opposed the ruling and 40 percent supported it.

Rather than muting America's long-running and emotional debate over abortion, Erwin Chemerinsky, dean of the University of California, Berkeley, School of Law, believes the court's ruling will increase division. "The Court's overruling *Roe* is not going to end the debate or the intense political controversy over abortion. Quite the contrary, it will intensify it as it will become the dominant issue in countless elections for Congress, for state legislatures, for city councils, and for judgeships,"[6] he says.

CHAPTER ONE

The History of Abortion Rights

The debate over abortion rights is a relatively recent issue in US history. In fact, until the mid-1800s, abortion was widespread and largely stigma-free for American women. It was not until the late 1800s and early 1900s that the push to criminalize abortion emerged.

A Widespread Practice

In the 1700s and early 1800s, pregnancy, childbirth, and women's health in general were widely viewed as women's issues. Women shared knowledge and information with each other. Midwives, rather than male doctors, usually cared for pregnant women and delivered babies. These attitudes and practices allowed women to control their health care. "It gave them a space to make their own decisions about their reproductive health,"[7] says Lauren MacIvor Thompson, a women's rights and public health historian.

At the time, there were few abortion laws in the United States. Abortions in the first trimester of pregnancy were relatively easy to obtain and carried little stigma. Newspapers advertised herbal remedies to cure "obstructed menses," a reference to a missed period, which is often an early sign of pregnancy. Although the Catholic Church disapproved of abortion, church officials viewed it as evidence of premarital sex, not murder.

During that period, abortion access was guided by British law, which relied on "quickening" to determine the legality of abortion. Quickening is the point in pregnancy when a woman can feel a fetus's movements, usually around twenty-two to twenty-four weeks of gestation. Without modern pregnancy tests and ultrasounds, quickening was the only way to confirm a pregnancy in the 1700s. American society did not recognize a fetus as the start of a new life until quickening occurred.

The main reasons women decided to terminate a pregnancy during this era included the lack of reliable contraception, the stigma of having a child outside of marriage, and the dangers of childbirth. Before quickening, women who did not want to have a baby could try to end a pregnancy by taking herbal concoctions to bring on menstruation. They might mix the herbs themselves or buy herbal medicines from local apothecaries. While these herbal concoctions sometimes worked to induce an abortion, they could also lead to poisoning. If the attempt to induce abortion made her sick enough, a hospital would sometimes perform a surgical abortion. A woman also could seek the advice of a midwife to help end a pregnancy. During this time, abortions were widely practiced. Some historians estimate that up to 35 percent of pregnancies in the 1800s were deliberately terminated.

Criminalization of Abortion

States began enacting abortion laws in the 1800s mainly in response to the poisonings caused by unsafe herbal remedies. Connecticut passed the country's first abortion law in 1821. The law punished anyone who provided or took a substance to terminate a pregnancy after quickening.

In the mid-1800s, doctors increasingly argued that male physicians, not female midwives, should care for women in pregnancy and manage their reproductive health. Male doctors also began to condemn abortion. In 1857 gynecologist Horatio Storer argued that abortion was immoral and interfered with nature. As founder of the Gynaecological Society of Boston, the first medical society for gynecology, Storer had broad influence on matters involving women's

Carol's Story

In 1965 twenty-two-year-old Carol Deanow was pregnant. She never considered having the baby, and she asked a friend for the name of someone who could perform an abortion. "Her friend knew a friend who knew a friend who had accompanied somebody to one; it was that kind of underground network," says Deanow. She gathered the $300 for the abortion and traveled from Baltimore to Washington, DC, for the illegal procedure. "We went to a small office and the person who carried it out was an MD. I was fortunate but it still felt very illegal. The room wasn't sterile, like an operating room, but it was clean and professional. I remember almost nothing about the procedure except the doctor saying, 'Don't make any noise.' And that it was painful, there was no anesthesia," she says. After the procedure, Deanow returned to her college dorm and told everyone she had the flu. Afterward, she felt relieved that the pregnancy was over. But she also felt a lot of guilt and ended up seeing a psychiatrist to work through her emotions.

Quoted in Candice Pires and Clare Considine, "'I Got in the Car and He Blindfolded Me. I Was Willing to Risk Death': Five Women on Abortions Before *Roe*," *The Guardian* (Manchester, UK), June 16, 2022. www.theguardian.com.

reproductive health. He believed abortion caused derangement in women and should be viewed as a serious crime. Storer led fellow doctors in a campaign to make abortion illegal in every state.

By the early 1900s every US state had passed antiabortion laws, many of which made abortion a felony. Although some of these laws made exceptions for pregnancies that threatened the mother's life or in cases of rape, only doctors were allowed to decide which circumstances justified an abortion. These laws made it more difficult for women to access safe abortions. While prosecutions of the women themselves were rare, the providers who performed the procedure could be sentenced to years in prison. "The legal punishments in place absolutely had a chilling effect," says MacIvor Thompson. "And yet, just like a hundred years earlier, women still sought them frequently."[8]

Abortion Goes Underground

With abortion outlawed, women who were desperate to end a pregnancy turned to unregulated, unsafe methods and unqualified practitioners. In the 1950s and 1960s, up to 1.2 million women had abortions each year, according to the Guttmacher Institute, a reproductive health research and policy organization. Black market doctors illegally provided abortion medications and surgical abortions for women who could afford to pay. Other women attempted to terminate pregnancies themselves. Jennifer Holland, assistant professor of US history at the University of Oklahoma, says, "The problem with the black market is that sometimes you would get doctors with degrees who were up on the latest medicine. Sometimes you would get midwives, but a lot of times you would unfortunately get total opportunists. And it was often very hard to figure out which of those you were seeing."[9]

Without regulation, abortions were often unsafe and could quickly become deadly. In 1930, according to the Guttmacher Institute, twenty-seven hundred women were reported to have died from illegal abortions. The introduction of antibiotics in the 1940s helped decrease abortion-related deaths. However, historians believe the actual deaths due to illegal abortions have always been higher than reported.

Calls for Change

In the 1960s Americans began to call for changes to abortion laws. "Illegal abortion became a public health crisis. You have thousands of women dying every year from unsafe back-alley abortions,"[10] says Kimberly Hamlin, professor of history at Miami University in Oxford, Ohio. These largely preventable deaths could no longer be ignored.

Many people—including activists, doctors, lawyers, and clergy members—called for states to repeal abortion laws. Organizations such as the American Medical Association and the American Bar Association joined the push to decriminalize abortion.

Slowly, states began to amend their laws to loosen abortion restrictions. In 1967 Colorado became the first state to ease its abortion laws, allowing abortion to protect the mother's physical and mental health, in cases of rape or incest, or if the fetus had severe birth defects. Several other states followed, including California in 1967 and New York in 1970.

Roe v. Wade

In 1970 a lawsuit in Texas challenged that state's abortion restrictions. At the time, abortion was illegal in Texas unless performed to save the mother's life. The lawsuit was filed by a pregnant, unmarried woman called Jane Roe in court documents (to preserve privacy) but later revealed to be Norma McCorvey. Roe's lawyers

In 1970 Norma McCorvey filed a lawsuit that challenged a Texas law that restricted a woman's access to abortion. To protect her privacy, she was known in court documents as Jane Roe. She later said she had been paid for her antiabortion sentiments.

argued that Texas abortion law invaded her right to liberty under the Fourteenth Amendment to the US Constitution, which prohibits states from depriving any person of life, liberty, or property without due process of law. They also argued that the Texas law infringed on her privacy rights—marital, familial, and sexual privacy—guaranteed by the Bill of Rights. These rights, they argued, allowed a woman to end a pregnancy at any time, for any reason, using any method.

Texas defended its abortion law and asserted that states have an interest in safeguarding health, maintaining medical standards, and protecting unborn lives. The state claimed that a fetus is a person protected by the Fourteenth Amendment and that protecting life from conception is a state interest.

The lawsuit, known as *Roe v. Wade*, made its way through the courts and eventually reached the US Supreme Court. In 1973 the Supreme Court issued its landmark ruling. By a vote of 7–2, the court had made abortion legal nationwide. The court interpreted the US Constitution's Fourteenth Amendment and determined that it provides a fundamental right to privacy that includes a person's right to chose whether to have an abortion.

However, the court also determined that abortion rights are not unlimited and must be balanced against the government's interest in protecting life and unborn life. To do this, the court devised a sys-

Kailey's Viewpoint

Kailey Cornett is twenty-eight years old and lives in Tennessee. She is the chief executive of Hope Clinic for Women, a center that provides services and support for pregnant women who choose to have their babies. Cornett became inspired to help women with unplanned pregnancies after attending a Christian youth conference as a teenager. In high school Cornett volunteered at a pregnancy resource center in Arizona. In college she obtained a degree in nonprofit management with the goal of leading her own center one day. Cornett believes that she can care for women and still be true to her Christian faith. At her clinic, she does provide some forms of birth control to patients. However, she is in favor of Tennessee's abortion ban with no exceptions for rape and incest. "I'm a firm believer that trauma leads to trauma. [A woman] ending the life of that child will not make her pain go away," she says.

Quoted in Ruth Graham, "'The Pro-Life Generation': Young Women Fight Against Abortion Rights," *New York Times*, July 3, 2022. www.nytimes.com.

tem to divide pregnancy into three twelve-week trimesters. In the first trimester, the court said, states cannot restrict abortion beyond requiring it to be performed by a licensed doctor. During the second trimester, a state may regulate abortion if reasonably related to the mother's health. In the third trimester, the court determined that the state's interest in protecting the unborn life outweighed the mother's right to privacy. As a result, states could ban abortions at this stage, except when necessary to save the life or health of the mother.

The *Roe v. Wade* decision was enormously significant across the country. The ruling changed the way states could regulate abortion. It also determined that the right to privacy, guaranteed by the Constitution, covered abortion rights.

Antiabortion Movement Begins

After *Roe*, people who opposed abortion began to organize against legalized abortion. "It was a very small movement, largely made up of white Catholics and a smattering of other religious people in the 1970s," says Jennifer Holland. "At this time, they're really developing these arguments that would carry the movement forward. They argue not only that the fetus is a life, but this is also a rights campaign, comparing legal abortion to genocide akin to the Holocaust."[11]

In the 1970s and 1980s, the antiabortion movement grew as more people, including evangelical Christians, joined. The Republican Party added an antiabortion plank to the party platform in 1976. Abortion became a partisan issue, with Republicans and Democrats on opposite sides.

Challenges to Abortion Rights

After *Roe v. Wade*, abortion opponents urged state lawmakers to pass laws restricting abortion. States including Louisiana, Nebraska, and Texas did this. In a series of cases over the next several decades, the Supreme Court ruled on whether some of those laws violated a woman's constitutional right to privacy. The

Antiabortion protesters demonstrate outside the US Supreme Court, demanding that Roe v. Wade be overturned.

court found many of the restrictions unconstitutional. However, the court allowed some laws to remain, including state and federal bans on funding for abortions and the requirement for minors to obtain parental consent or notify their parents before having an abortion.

In 1992 the court reaffirmed the original rationale for *Roe*, which is that the constitutional right to privacy covers women's medical decisions, including the decision to obtain an abortion. In that case, *Planned Parenthood of Southeastern Pennsylvania v. Casey*, the Supreme Court made one significant change to the law, however. It replaced the three-trimester framework established in *Roe* with a standard based on fetal viability, which is the ability of a fetus to survive outside the womb. It also declared that restrictions were allowed as long as they did not impose an undue burden. This change made it easier for states to pass more restrictive abortion laws, such as laws that required pre-abortion counseling, waiting periods, and parental consent for minors.

By the 2000s the antiabortion movement had grown in size and influence. Antiabortion groups urged conservative politicians to pass new restrictive state abortion laws that could present a legal challenge to *Roe v. Wade*. In addition, the composition of the Supreme Court itself had changed. After the confirmation of Justice Amy Coney Barrett in 2020, the nine-member court included six conservative justices who were considered to be more likely to rule against abortion rights and *Roe*. For example, Alabama passed one of the strictest abortion laws in the country in 2019. The law banned abortions at every stage of pregnancy, with exceptions only when there is a severe risk to the mother's life. This law represented a direct challenge to *Roe v. Wade*. "Our position is just simply that the unborn child is a person, and the bill goes directly to that," Rich Wingo, a member of the Alabama House of Representatives, said shortly after the law's passage. "Courts can do—and have done—many things good and bad, but we would hope and pray that they would go and that they would overturn *Roe*."[12]

> "Our position is just simply that the unborn child is a person."[12]
>
> —Rich Wingo, member of the Alabama House of Representative

By this time, however, a Mississippi law that banned most abortions after fifteen weeks of pregnancy was already moving through the courts. In May 2021 the Supreme Court announced it would hear arguments in that case. The ruling that would eventually be issued by the court would be as consequential as any in the US history of abortion.

CHAPTER TWO

The Ruling That Overturned *Roe*

Mississippi lawmakers passed the Gestational Age Act in 2018. The law banned all abortions after fifteen weeks of gestational age, which was about eight weeks earlier than *Roe* allowed. The law only permitted a few exceptions to the ban, such as when the mother experienced a medical emergency or the fetus had a severe abnormality. Lawmakers justified the new law by asserting that a fetus has made significant physical development by this point. They also contended that abortions performed after fifteen weeks increase risks to the mother. "We are saving more of the unborn than any state in America, and what better thing we could do,"[13] Mississippi governor Phil Bryant said as he signed the law.

Challenged in Court

Less than an hour after the bill became law, abortion rights supporters challenged it. Jackson Women's Health Organization, the state's only abortion clinic, filed a complaint in federal court to block the new law. Lawyers for the clinic argued the law directly challenged *Roe v. Wade* and created an unconstitutional restriction on abortion providers. After an emergency hearing, a federal court agreed and blocked enforcement of the law.

The case moved to a federal appeals court, where the abortion clinic provided evidence that a fifteen-week-old fetus could not survive outside the womb and thus did not meet the fetal viability rule established by *Casey*. The appeals court agreed with the lower court's ruling and left in place its action blocking enforcement of the law. The appeals court said Mississippi had presented no evidence to prove fetal viability at fifteen weeks. Mississippi appealed that decision to the Supreme Court. In May 2021 the Supreme Court agreed to hear the Mississippi case, *Dobbs v. Jackson Women's Health Organization*.

Mississippi Makes Its Case Before the Supreme Court

Both sides prepared briefs for the Supreme Court, in which they detailed the facts and history of the case, the issues to be decided, and the reasons why the court should rule in their favor. In its brief, Mississippi asked the court to overturn the appeals court ruling. But there was more. That state asked the court to overturn both the *Roe* and *Casey* decisions.

In *Dobbs*, Mississippi argued that the court should overturn *Roe* and *Casey* because the decisions in both cases were egregiously wrong and undemocratic, since abortion rights are not explicitly addressed in the Constitution. Mississippi asserted that decisions on abortion rights should be made by the states, not in the courts. It argued that the states have an interest in protecting the life of the fetus, the health of the mother, and the integrity of medical professionals. Mississippi attorney general Lynn Fitch told the Supreme Court justices that abortion "needs to be given back to the states. The unelected judiciary don't need to be making those decisions for us. . . . We all elect our legislators . . . and then you know what? They're accountable."[14]

Arguments Against Mississippi's Law

Lawyers for Jackson Women's Health Organization argued that Mississippi's law was unconstitutional—that it conflicted with abortion rights and standards previously established and then

In May 2021 the Supreme Court (pictured) agreed to hear a case from Mississippi, Dobbs v. Jackson Women's Health Organization.

upheld by the court. "Mississippi's ban on abortion two months before viability is flatly unconstitutional under decades of precedent. For a state to take control of a woman's body and demand that she go through pregnancy and childbirth, with all the physical risks and life-altering consequences that brings, is a fundamental deprivation of her liberty,"[15] Julie Rikelman, senior litigation director for the Center for Reproductive Rights, told the justices on behalf of the Jackson Women's Health Organization.

Rikelman argued that the right to abortion was essential for women's liberty, equality, and health. The Mississippi law, she stated, would have a significant adverse effect in all of these areas. "Eliminating or reducing the right to abortion will propel women backward. Two generations have now relied on this right, and one out of every four women makes the decision to end a pregnancy,"[16] she said.

> "For a state to take control of a woman's body and demand that she go through pregnancy and childbirth, with all the physical risks and life-altering consequences that brings, is a fundamental deprivation of her liberty."[15]
>
> —Julie Rikelman, senior litigation director for the Center for Reproductive Rights

Elizabeth Prelogar, US solicitor general, also presented arguments to the court on behalf of the federal government and in support of Jackson Women's Health Organization. She warned of the devastating effect overturning long-standing law would have on women and families. Prelogar said:

> The real-world effects of overruling *Roe* and *Casey* would be severe and swift. Nearly half of the states already have or are expected to enact bans on abortion at all stages of pregnancy. If this court renounces the liberty interest recognized in *Roe* and reaffirmed in *Casey*, it would be an unprecedented contraction of individual rights. . . . The court has never revoked a right that is so fundamental to so many.[17]

The Decision

On June 24, 2022, the Supreme Court issued its ruling. The justices voted 6–3 to permit Mississippi's law banning abortions after fifteen weeks of gestation. Then in a stunning reversal, they also found in a 5–4 decision that the US Constitution does not protect the right to abortion, effectively overturning *Roe v. Wade*.

> "The Constitution makes no reference to abortion, and no such right is implicitly protected by any constitutional provision."[18]
>
> —Samuel Alito, US Supreme Court justice, in the majority opinion for *Dobbs v. Jackson Women's Health Organization*

Justice Samuel Alito wrote the majority opinion. He was joined by Justices Clarence Thomas, Neil Gorsuch, Brett Kavanaugh, and Amy Coney Barrett. In the opinion, Alito noted that the issue of abortion was complex and that Americans held deeply conflicting views. He also stated that the Constitution did not provide a right to abortion. Therefore, in the majority's opinion, all prior cases that established abortion rights, including *Roe v. Wade*, were wrong from the start. "The Constitution makes no reference to abortion, and no such right is implicitly protected by any constitutional provision,"[18] he wrote.

The Majority Opinion

Below are excerpts from the majority opinion in the *Dobbs* case, which overturned the constitutional right to abortion.

"The Constitution makes no reference to abortion, and no such right is implicitly protected by any constitutional provision, including the one on which the defenders of *Roe* and *Casey* now chiefly rely—the Due Process Clause of the Fourteenth Amendment. That provision has been held to guarantee some rights that are not mentioned in the Constitution, but any such right must be 'deeply rooted in this Nation's history and tradition' and 'implicit in the concept of ordered liberty.'"

"The right to abortion does not fall within this category. Until the latter part of the 20th century, such a right was entirely unknown in American law."

"Not only was there no support for such a constitutional right until shortly before *Roe*, but abortion had long been a *crime* in every single State. . . . Abortion was criminal in at least some stages of pregnancy and was regarded as unlawful and could have very serious consequences at all stages."

"Abortion presents a profound moral question. The Constitution does not prohibit the citizens of each State from regulating or prohibiting abortion. *Roe* and *Casey* arrogated [usurped] that authority. We now overrule those decisions and return that authority to the people and their elected representatives."

Dobbs v. Jackson Women's Health Organization, No. 19-1392, 597 U.S. ___ (2022).

The majority opinion is based on a conservative principle called originalism. Originalism is a belief that a text such as the Constitution should be interpreted in a way that follows how it would have been intended or understood at the time it was written. In comparison, a more liberal interpretation views the Constitution as a living document whose meaning adapts and evolves as society evolves. Following the principles of originalism, the majority opinion notes that the right to abortion is not explicitly stated in the Constitution. Although the court has granted

The Dissenting Opinion

Below are excerpts from the dissenting opinion in the *Dobbs* case, which accused the court of betraying its guiding principles and turning women into second-class citizens.

"For half a century, *Roe v. Wade*, and *Planned Parenthood of Southeastern Pa. v. Casey*, have protected the liberty and equality of women. *Roe* held, and *Casey* reaffirmed, that the Constitution safeguards a woman's right to decide for herself whether to bear a child."

"One result of today's decision is certain: the curtailment of women's rights, and of their status as free and equal citizens. Yesterday, the Constitution guaranteed that a woman confronted with an unplanned pregnancy could (within reasonable limits) make her own decision about whether to bear a child, with all the life-transforming consequences that act involves. And in thus safeguarding each woman's reproductive freedom, the Constitution also protected '[t]he ability of women to participate equally in [this Nation's] economic and social life.' But no longer. As of today, this Court holds, a State can always force a woman to give birth, prohibiting even the earliest abortions. A State can thus transform what, when freely undertaken, is a wonder into what, when forced, may be a nightmare. . . . The Constitution will, today's majority holds, provide no shield, despite its guarantees of liberty and equality for all."

"With sorrow—for this Court, but more, for the many millions of American women who have today lost a fundamental constitutional protection—we dissent."

Dobbs v. Jackson Women's Health Organization, No. 19-1392, 597 U.S. ___ (2022).

constitutional protection to some rights not expressly stated in the Constitution, known as unenumerated rights, Alito said that abortion does not qualify as an unenumerated right because it is not deeply rooted in the country's history and traditions. Alito justified the reversal of *Roe v. Wade* by noting that the decision was egregiously wrong from the beginning and based on an analysis that was beyond a reasonable interpretation of the Constitution.

In overruling prior abortion rights decisions, the Supreme Court returned the power to regulate abortion to the states. The ruling overturned nearly fifty years of legal precedent, which had repeatedly held up to challenges over the years. Joanne Rosen, a health law and policy expert at the Johns Hopkins Bloomberg School of Public Health, says, "What is extraordinary in this case is that, perhaps for the first time, the Supreme Court departed from precedent not to recognize a right it previously neglected but rather to remove one it previously protected. It *deconstitutionalized* a longstanding right. This is an astonishing moment and an astonishing use of the court's authority."[19]

The Dissent

Four justices—Chief Justice John Roberts, Stephen Breyer, Sonia Sotomayor, and Elena Kagan—disagreed with the court's decision to overturn the constitutional right to abortion. Three justices—Breyer, Sotomayor, and Kagan—wrote a joint dissenting opinion, outlining their response to the majority opinion. In the dissent, the justices accused the court of betraying its guiding principles and turning women into second-class citizens. The justices wrote:

> After today, young women will come of age with fewer rights than their mothers and grandmothers had. The majority accomplishes that result without so much as considering how women have relied on the right to choose or what it means to take that right away. The majority's refusal even to consider the life-altering consequences of reversing *Roe* and *Casey* is a stunning indictment of its decision.[20]

The dissenting justices noted that in previous Supreme Court decisions, the court had recognized that women must be able to make the decision for themselves on whether to have a child.

"Respecting a woman as an autonomous being, and granting her full equality, meant giving her substantial choice over this most personal and most consequential of all life decisions,"[21] the justices wrote.

The justices acknowledged that this fundamental right had some limits and was not absolute. They cited the fetal viability standard as an example of reasonable limits that balanced the rights of the woman and the rights of states to protect the unborn child. However, with the *Dobbs* decision, the dissenting justices accused the majority of only considering the states' rights. "Today, the Court discards that balance," the justices wrote. "It says that from the very moment of fertilization, a woman has no rights to speak of."[22]

The dissenting justices argued against the majority's originalist interpretation that the Constitution does not provide for the right to an abortion. They noted that women were not considered full members of society at the time of the country's founding. Therefore, it is not surprising that the nation's founders did not understand the importance of reproductive rights for women's liberty and ability to be equal members of society. "When the majority says that we must read our foundational charter as viewed at the time of ratification (except that we may also check it against the Dark Ages), it consigns women to second-class citizenship,"[23] the justices wrote.

The Supreme Court's 2022 decision to uphold Mississippi's abortion ban and overturn *Roe v. Wade* sent shock waves across the country. People who had lived for decades under *Roe*'s protections now faced uncertainty. Depending on which state a person lived in, access to reproductive health and abortion suddenly became much more difficult.

CHAPTER THREE

The States React

The reaction was swift when the *Dobbs* ruling returned the authority to regulate abortion to the states. Some states reverted to decades-old laws that banned abortion or newer trigger laws that immediately went into effect. Other states moved quickly to enact laws protecting access to abortion.

Abortion Bans and Trigger Laws

Several states had been preparing for the day when the Supreme Court might strike down *Roe* and end federal abortion protections. Over the years thirteen states—Arkansas, Idaho, Kentucky, Louisiana, Mississippi, Missouri, North Dakota, Oklahoma, South Dakota, Tennessee, Texas, Utah, and Wyoming—had passed trigger laws that would take effect if and when the Supreme Court overturned *Roe v. Wade*. Within hours of the *Dobbs* decision's release, trigger laws took effect in six of those states—Arkansas, Kentucky, Louisiana, Missouri, South Dakota, and Utah.

The details of the trigger laws varied by state. Most states with trigger laws banned abortion entirely. Some allowed limited exceptions such as in cases of rape or incest. Some states, like Tennessee, prohibited all abortions except to prevent death or substantial injury to the mother. Several states, such as Tennessee and Kentucky, made it a felony for a doctor to perform an illegal abortion. In Mississippi a trigger law banned all abortions ten days after *Roe* was overturned, with the only exception being for cases of rape that had been reported to the police.

In Missouri, just minutes after the *Dobbs* decision was announced, Governor Mike Parson signed a proclamation enacting the state's trigger law. It prohibits doctors from performing most abortions and turns what was an accepted medical procedure into a felony. Anyone convicted of breaking the law can be sentenced to up to fifteen years in prison. Under Missouri law there is a limited exception for medical emergencies but no exceptions for rape or incest. "Nothing in the text, history, or tradition of the United States Constitution gave un-elected federal judges authority to regulate abortion. We are happy that the U.S. Supreme Court has corrected this error and returned power to the people and the states to make these decisions,"[24] said Parson in a statement.

> "Nothing in the text, history, or tradition of the United States Constitution gave un-elected federal judges authority to regulate abortion."[24]
>
> —Mike Parson, governor of Missouri

A similar trigger law took effect in Oklahoma. At a news conference, Attorney General John O'Connor warned of the state's intention to prosecute offenders. "Oklahoma's law is very clear now. Law enforcement is now activated in respect to any effort to aid, abet or solicit any abortions."[25] An additional law to increase penalties to ten years in prison and levy a fine of $100,000 for performing an abortion became effective in late August 2022.

Pre-*Roe* Bans

Four other states—Arizona, Michigan, West Virginia, and Wisconsin—had decades-old abortion bans still on the books from pre-*Roe* days. While *Roe* stood, these bans were unconstitutional and could not be enforced. However, once *Roe* was overturned, these laws became immediately enforceable. For example, in Arizona a 1901 law that criminalized abortion was reinstated after the *Dobbs* decision. Under the law, anyone who performs an abortion or helps a woman get one can be charged with a felony punishable by two to five years in prison. There is an exception to the abortion ban when it is necessary to save a woman's life.

Several other states enacted laws that restrict abortion without banning it entirely. Some of these laws had been on hold until the *Dobbs* ruling. In Georgia a 2019 law bans most abortions after six weeks of pregnancy. That law had been blocked by federal courts. However, after *Dobbs* a federal appeals court panel allowed the law to go into effect. The *Dobbs* ruling overturning *Roe v. Wade* "makes clear that no right to abortion exists under the

US Abortion Laws in the Aftermath of the *Dobbs* Decision

In the aftermath of the Supreme Court ruling that overturned *Roe v. Wade*, states have responded by reinstating old laws and passing new ones. This has created a confusing mix of restrictions and protections. Some states have banned abortions and allowed few or no exceptions. Other states have passed laws that protect access to abortions. More changes are likely. This map, from the reproductive health research and policy organization Guttmacher Institute, shows the types of policies that were in effect as of September 5, 2022.

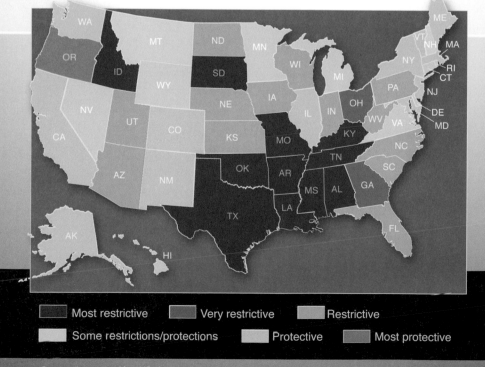

Most restrictive   Very restrictive   Restrictive

Some restrictions/protections   Protective   Most protective

Source: "Interactive Map: US Abortion Policies and Access After Roe," Guttmacher Institute, September 5, 2022. https://states.guttmacher.org/policies.

Blocking the Bans

Abortion providers are filing lawsuits to halt state abortion bans that went into effect after the Supreme Court's reversal of *Roe v. Wade*. In West Virginia, abortion providers sued the state, arguing that its nineteenth-century pre-*Roe* abortion ban conflicts with more recent state laws and violates the state constitution. A judge agreed and in July 2022 blocked the ban from taking effect. The decision has been appealed. In September 2022, however, West Virginia lawmakers passed a new law that bans nearly all abortions. And in Wyoming, a judge blocked the state's trigger law, which banned all abortions with exceptions for medical emergencies, rape, and incest. The judge agreed with abortion providers who argued that it was too vague and did not provide any guidance for providers to determine whether a patient can legally have an abortion.

Constitution, so Georgia may prohibit them,"[26] wrote Chief Judge William H. Pryor Jr., one of the panel's judges.

The Georgia law bans all abortions once a doctor can detect a fetal heartbeat, typically around six weeks of gestation. There are limited exceptions if a mother's life is at risk, if she faces serious harm, or in cases of rape or incest if a police report exists.

New Abortion Bans and Restrictions

Other states have moved quickly to pass new abortion bans and restrictions. In August 2022 Indiana became the first state to pass a new abortion ban after the *Dobbs* ruling. Indiana's new law bans abortions except when the woman's life is at risk, in cases of rape or incest, and in cases of fatal fetal anomalies. Doctors who perform abortions and clinics where they occur face loss of their licenses.

Large employers in Indiana expressed concerns about the new law. Eli Lilly, a pharmaceutical company with more than ten thousand employees in Indianapolis, said it was concerned that the law could negatively impact the company's ability to attract talented workers. "While we have expanded our employee health plan coverage to include travel for reproductive services unavailable locally, that may not be enough for some current and potential employees,"[27] the company states. As a result, the company plans to explore future growth outside Indiana.

Members of the Indiana House of Representatives meet to debate a law banning most abortions. In August 2022 Indiana became the first state to pass a ban on abortions following the Supreme Court's overturning of Roe v. Wade.

Some states are exploring potential laws to restrict citizens from traveling to another state for abortion care. They have proposed penalizing those who help a woman obtain an abortion in another state. Actions such as driving a woman to the appointment or funding her travel expenses are among those that could incur a penalty. Some states are looking into ways to penalize out-of-state providers for performing abortion procedures on their state's residents. As of late 2022, however, no such laws had been passed.

Protecting Abortion Rights

While some states have enacted abortion bans, other states are working just as quickly to preserve abortion rights. In July 2022 the New York state legislature passed a constitutional amendment guaranteeing access to abortion and contraception in that state. It was the first step in a multiyear process to amend the state's constitution. "We refuse to stand idly by while the Supreme Court attacks the rights of New Yorkers,"[28] New York governor Kathy Hochul said shortly after the legislature took action.

> "We refuse to stand idly by while the Supreme Court attacks the rights of New Yorkers."[28]
>
> —Kathy Hochul, governor of New York

New Jersey has also passed new laws protecting abortion access, abortion providers, and people who travel to that state to obtain an abortion. In anticipation of a Supreme Court ruling overturning *Roe*, in January 2022 New Jersey lawmakers enshrined the right to obtain an abortion in state law. They also passed two new laws shortly after the *Dobbs* decision. One law protects doctors who perform abortions and patients who obtain abortions in New Jersey from being extradited to another state where abortion is illegal. The second law prohibits New Jersey state agencies from helping or releasing information to other states for criminal abortion investigations. "While others throughout the country are revoking a woman's right to reproductive freedom, New Jersey will continue to defend this fundamental right in our state,"[29] Governor Phil Murphy said shortly after the passage of the new laws.

Connecticut legislators have also passed a new law protecting abortion rights. That law, which went into effect in July 2022, protects abortion providers as well as patients who travel to Connecticut for abortion care. It also made abortion services more accessible by expanding the type of medical personnel allowed to perform abortion procedures.

> "While others throughout the country are revoking a woman's right to reproductive freedom, New Jersey will continue to defend this fundamental right in our state."[29]
>
> —Phil Murphy, governor of New Jersey

Fetal Personhood

The questions of when life begins and when a fetus has rights are at the center of the abortion debate. A movement to grant fetuses the same legal rights as anyone else, known as fetal personhood, is gaining interest from some antiabortion activists. Currently, people have legal rights from the time they are born. Those who support fetal personhood believe these rights should be conferred from the moment of conception. Those who hold this view consider the fetus to be a separate and constitutionally protected person from the woman who carries the fetus in her uterus. If fetal personhood were to gain recognition as a legal standard in the United States, it would not only end all abortions, it would also lead to classification of abortion as murder.

Abortion Sanctuaries

In the weeks before and after the *Dobbs* ruling, some states moved to create abortion sanctuaries, where people could come for reproductive care without fear of legal reprisals. Several states—including California, Colorado, Connecticut, Illinois, Massachusetts, and New York—have passed new laws and provided funds to help the growing number of patients traveling to their states for abortion procedures.

In California, lawmakers have introduced more than a dozen bills to expand access to abortions for residents and nonresidents. These bills would provide funding to clinics, help patients with travel expenses, and allow some trained nurses to perform abortion care with a doctor's supervision. State legislators also passed a constitutional amendment that was to appear on the November 2022 ballot. If approved by voters, Proposition 1 would establish the right to abortion and contraception in the state constitution. Shannon Olivieri Hovis, the director of the advocacy organization NARAL Pro-Choice California, says:

> We are addressing our provider shortages. We are addressing our access deserts. We are ensuring that people have the practical, logistical and financial support to get here. We are strengthening our provider network. We are doing all of the things that we need to do, and we are guaranteeing that they have privacy in their records and that they are not at risk of legal repercussions, providers or patients, in the state of California based on these hostile bans that we're going to see move forward.[30]

In Colorado, lawmakers are positioning the state to provide care for abortion seekers from nearby states, including Texas, Wyoming, and Utah. In April 2022 the state enacted the Reproductive Health Equity Act, which codifies protections for reproductive care, including abortion, in state law. The act also establishes

At a news conference, California governor Gavin Newsom displays a bill he signed, which shields abortion providers and volunteers from civil judgments from out-of-state courts.

that a fertilized egg, embryo, or fetus does not have personhood rights in Colorado. "In Colorado, we truly respect individual rights and freedoms," says Governor Jared Polis. "Women's right to choose is now protected in Colorado."[31] In addition, Colorado voters will decide in 2024 whether to add abortion rights to the state's constitution.

The Supreme Court's ruling in the *Dobbs* case and its reversal of *Roe v. Wade* sparked a flurry of activity from states nationwide. While some states implemented abortion bans and restrictions, others worked to expand access to safe, legal abortions.

CHAPTER FOUR

Feeling the Effects

When Chloe and her fiancé discovered that she was pregnant with their second child, they were thrilled. However, when Chloe had a routine ultrasound at twenty-one weeks, the doctor noticed some troubling signs with the fetus and sent her to a specialist. Chloe discovered that her baby had a condition that was incompatible with life. The doctors gave her several options. In Arizona, where she lives, abortions were not permitted after fifteen weeks. So Chloe could travel out of state for an abortion, or have a doctor induce labor prematurely, or let the baby pass away in utero and then expel it naturally. Around that time, the fetus began having seizure-like movements that Chloe could feel. She worried that the fetus was suffering, and she wanted to do the best thing for her unborn child. Chloe chose to induce labor as she thought it was the most compassionate choice and would allow her to hold her baby at least once. "I wanted to end her suffering in a peaceful way, and I wanted to spend some moments with her and be able to love on her,"[32] she says.

Chloe and her doctor planned to induce labor in June 2022. In the case of a nonviable pregnancy like Chloe's, the doctor stops the fetal heart and then induces delivery of the fetus. This procedure is technically considered an abortion. However, before the procedure could be done, the Supreme Court announced its decision to overturn *Roe*. Chloe's doctor called and told her he could no longer do the procedure, and her only choice if she did not want to travel out of state was to carry the baby until it died in the womb.

Suddenly, Chloe had few options. The *Dobbs* ruling overturning *Roe* triggered Arizona's pre-*Roe* abortion ban as well as a 2022 law that banned the procedure after fifteen weeks. Hospitals and doctors halted abortions amid the legal uncertainty over which state law would take precedence: the near-total pre-*Roe* ban or the fifteen-week ban. This forced Chloe to continue with her pregnancy even though she could feel the fetus having seizures and believed the baby was suffering. "I really can only describe it as feeling trapped. Not being able to choose what to do in regards to me and her, I just feel trapped and it's not fair to me or for anybody that's going through something like this," she says. Many people who know about Chloe's situation are surprised that she could not have an abortion. "People in my life are saying, 'This should be an exception.' 'I never thought about it this way.' 'I didn't know how it could affect people in a situation like yours,'" she says. By speaking out, Chloe hopes others will see how the court's ruling can affect ordinary people. "That's a good start to having people understand what the overturn really does,"[33] she says.

Abortion: A Common Procedure

Across the United States, abortion is common. In 2020 about one in five pregnancies ended in abortion. The vast majority of abortions, 93 percent, occurred in the first trimester of pregnancy, according to the Centers for Disease Control and Prevention (CDC). Fifty-six percent of abortions were performed surgically in a hospital or clinic, while 44 percent of patients used abortion medications to end a pregnancy. According to estimates from the Guttmacher Institute, a reproductive health research group, 25 percent of women will have an abortion in their lifetime.

The majority of abortion patients are young, unmarried women in their twenties. According to a June 2022 report from the Pew Research Center, in 2019, 57 percent of abortion patients were in their twenties, while 31 percent were in their thirties, and 9 percent were ages thirteen to nineteen. A majority of these women, 85 percent, were unmarried. For more than half (58 percent), it was their first time having an abortion.

The women who have abortions come from many different racial and ethnic backgrounds. Non-Hispanic Black women accounted for 38 percent of abortions in 2019, while 33 percent of abortions were non-Hispanic White women, 21 percent were Hispanic, and 7 percent identified as other races, according to CDC data. "There isn't one monolith demographic who get abortions. The same people who become pregnant and give birth are the same people who have abortions at different points in their lives,"[34] says Ushma Upadhyay, a professor with Advancing New Standards in Reproductive Health at the University of California, San Francisco. All of these women are now affected by the *Roe* reversal.

Many Different Reasons

Women who choose to have an abortion do so for various reasons. Some women decide to terminate a pregnancy because they are not emotionally ready or financially able to raise a child (or in some cases, to raise more children). When Casey Duran was twenty-four years old and working as a receptionist for fifteen dollars an hour, her birth control failed, and she became pregnant. She chose to terminate the pregnancy. "I knew I wasn't ready, and I tried to protect myself the best ways I thought. And it still happened. It can happen," she says. "I still think about how different my life would be if I didn't have access to a safe abortion. I would be living on assistance, raising a child on a minimum wage salary."[35]

Other women terminate a pregnancy because they do not want to bring a child into an abusive relationship. In some cases the pregnancy is the result of rape or incest. At age sixteen Hannah was raped by her boyfriend. A month later, she discovered that she was pregnant. "At the time, if he had found out that I was pregnant, he would have kidnapped me and the baby,"[36] she says. Hannah turned to Planned Parenthood for abortion care.

Sometimes women choose to terminate a wanted pregnancy due to health issues of the baby or the mother. If the baby has severe birth defects or a condition incompatible with life, the woman may choose to terminate rather than carry the fetus to term. Other times abortion is necessary to preserve the life and health of the mother.

Jill Hawkins, a clinical social worker in New York City, knows the difficulty of deciding to terminate a pregnancy to save her own life. In August 2021 Hawkins was diagnosed with chronic myeloid leukemia, a form of blood cancer. Hawkins's doctors prescribed medication to treat her cancer. Then in March 2022, Hawkins discovered that she was pregnant. She faced a difficult decision. The medication that was keeping her cancer under control was known to cause significant fetal abnormalities. Her oncologist gave her two choices. She could continue the pregnancy and switch to a different drug. The new treatment would be safer for the baby but more toxic to her. Her other choice was to get an abortion. "It's not a good idea for my health. Do I want to let go

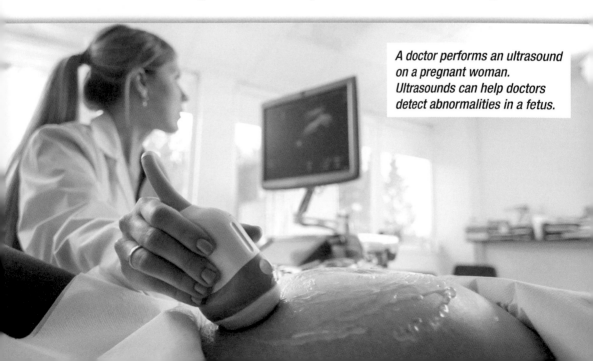

A doctor performs an ultrasound on a pregnant woman. Ultrasounds can help doctors detect abnormalities in a fetus.

of this pregnancy and be sad and grieve, or do I want to keep it and feel anxious and fearful of losing my life?" says Hawkins. After discussing the risks with her oncologist and family doctor, Hawkins chose to have an abortion. "It could have been a very difficult pregnancy. I could have lost my life. I could have had to make a really hard decision at 24 weeks," Hawkins says. "There were so many potential negatives attached to both choices. I just had to make the preferable of the two . . . choices I had."[37]

Confusion Reigns

American women have had the right to obtain an abortion for half a century. In the wake of the *Dobbs* ruling, many women were angry. Others were worried about their limited options. Doctors and medical providers were also confused about the changing scope of state laws and whether they could be sued or charged with a criminal offense for providing certain types of reproductive care.

In Louisiana in July 2022, Nancy Davis found out ten weeks into her pregnancy that her baby had a fatal condition called acrania, a rare disorder in which a fetus's skull does not form inside the womb. Doctors told her the child would die shortly after birth and recommended that she terminate the pregnancy. However, because of Louisiana's abortion ban and unclear guidance on the circumstances under which abortion is permitted, Woman's Hospital in Baton Rouge chose not to perform the

procedure. "Basically, they said I had to carry my baby to bury my baby," says Davis. "They seemed confused about the law and afraid of what would happen to them if they perform a criminal abortion, according to the law." Davis is speaking out about her situation because she does not want other women to go through her experience. "I want you to imagine what it's been like to continue this pregnancy for another six weeks after this diagnosis," Davis said at a news conference on the steps of the Louisiana State Capitol in Baton Rouge. "This is not fair to me, and it should not happen to any other woman,"[38] she says. In September 2022 Davis traveled to New York for an abortion.

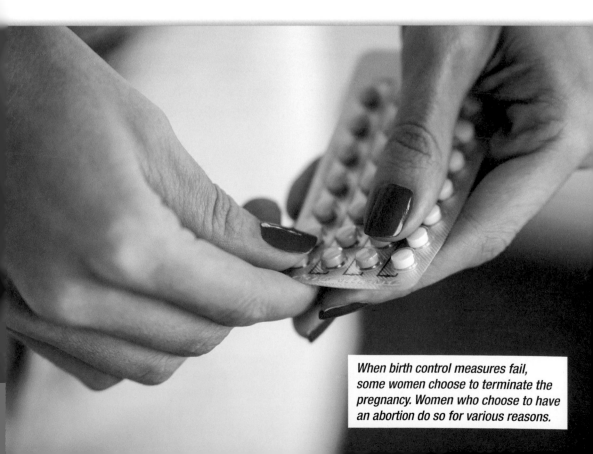

When birth control measures fail, some women choose to terminate the pregnancy. Women who choose to have an abortion do so for various reasons.

Caroline Isemann, a spokesperson for Woman's Hospital, said that navigating a nonviable pregnancy has become highly complicated post-*Roe*. "We look at each patient's individual circumstances and how to remain in compliance with all current state laws to the best of our ability," she says. "Even if a specific diagnosis falls under medically futile exceptions provided by (the Louisiana Department of Health), the laws addressing treatment methods are much more complex and seemingly contradictory."[39]

Confusion over new abortion laws and restrictions—and fear of prosecution—has disrupted standard reproductive medical care for some women—even when it risks their health. In Texas thirty-five-year-old Amanda had a first-trimester miscarriage in 2021. Her doctor performed a standard surgical procedure, called a dilation and curettage, to safely remove the nonviable fetal tissue in her uterus from the failed pregnancy. In 2022 Amanda suffered another first-trimester miscarriage. This time the hospital told her it could not perform the same procedure because it is also used for some abortions. Instead, she was sent home, where

Life of the Mother

In states that ban abortion but allow exceptions to save the mother's life, doctors and hospitals are increasingly being asked to determine at what point they can legally intervene. To protect themselves from being sued or charged with a crime, some hospitals have set up special panels of doctors and lawyers to determine whether a pregnancy can be terminated. Others require multiple doctors to sign off on a termination decision and document why an abortion is necessary. These added steps have delayed treatment and increased the risk of complications for pregnant women.

In Texas, which banned abortion after six weeks, a study of two hospitals reviewed the cases of twenty-eight women who faced serious complications mostly because the amniotic sac surrounding the baby broke prematurely. Because of the abortion ban, these women were not allowed to have an abortion even though the probability of their babies surviving was extremely low. The women were forced to continue with their pregnancies until their bodies naturally expelled the fetal tissue, which increased their risk of infection and complications. Of the twenty-eight women in the Texas study, more than half experienced significant medical problems, such as infection and hemorrhaging. One woman's complications led to a hysterectomy. In all but one of the cases, the fetus died.

she spent hours in severe pain as her body tried to expel the fetal tissue. She moved to the bathtub and cried. "The bathtub water is just dark red. For 48 hours, it was like a constant heavy bleed and big clots," she says. "It was so different from my first experience where they [medical staff] were so nice and so comforting, to now just feeling alone and terrified."[40]

Delays in removing nonviable tissue from pregnancy can become life threatening for the woman and lead to hemorrhaging, infection, and blood poisoning, or sepsis. "In this post-*Roe* world, women with miscarriages may die,"[41] says Monica Saxena, an emergency medicine physician at Stanford Hospital.

The effects were felt nationwide when the Supreme Court overturned *Roe v. Wade*. Women encountered barriers to reproductive care, including abortions, which had been accessible only months earlier. Medical professionals, hospitals, and clinics faced uncertainty over what procedures were permitted and what could get them in legal trouble. The changing rules have confused many people throughout the country. For many, this confusion has had a negative impact on women's health care.

CHAPTER FIVE

The Scramble for Abortion Alternatives

Women have always needed abortion care, whether it was legal or not. After the *Dobbs* ruling, many abortion clinics and providers canceled previously scheduled procedures and new appointments because they feared criminal prosecution. As many states have restricted or eliminated access to abortion, women have begun turning to alternative ways to get the care they need. "Bans, criminalization and bounty hunter laws, especially without exceptions even for rape and incest or the life of the mother, will not stop abortions,"[42] says Senator Ben Cardin of Maryland.

Services Come to a Halt

When the Supreme Court overturned *Roe v. Wade* on June 24, 2022, the Houston Women's Reproductive Services clinic was in the middle of a typical day of appointments. Within minutes of the ruling, however, everything stopped. The twenty women booked for appointments that day, some already sitting in the waiting room, would not receive abortion care. The overturning of *Roe* triggered a law in Texas that outlawed most abortions, and for this reason, abortion providers could immediately face criminal penalties, including jail time, for performing abortions.

The staff told patients the clinic could no longer provide abortion care. One woman had driven hundreds of miles for her appointment because the only clinic in her home state of Mississippi could not see her for several weeks. As they learned the news, several women walked out of the clinic in tears. Victoria, age twenty-five and five weeks pregnant, broke into tears when the clinic called to cancel her appointment. She met with clinic staff to discuss her options, including ordering abortion pills online or traveling to a state where she could still legally get an abortion. To travel, she would have to find childcare, ask for time off work, and pay for travel expenses. "I'm five weeks, there's no heartbeat." And still, she says, "my rights were just taken."[43]

> "Bans, criminalization and bounty hunter laws, especially without exceptions even for rape and incest or the life of the mother, will not stop abortions."[42]
>
> —Ben Cardin, US senator from Maryland

Crossing State Lines

When their appointments were abruptly canceled and clinics closed, some women made plans to travel to other states where abortion was still legal. Alicia, age twenty-four, could no longer obtain an abortion in her home state of Texas, so she traveled more than 600 miles (966 km) to a clinic in New Mexico. A support group helped Alicia pay for her travel, including a plane ticket, rental car, and motel costs. Without their support, Alicia says, "I probably wouldn't be here right now. I would have had to use all my savings." Alicia is angry at the abortion bans in Texas and other states. Antiabortion lawmakers "are not going to help me raise this baby," she says. "What if I was homeless? Would they expect me to live on the street with it?"[44]

Medical providers are also traveling across state lines to provide abortion care. Within hours of the *Dobbs* ruling, abortion providers in Wisconsin began shutting down because of a 173-year-old law that banned the procedure unless a woman's life was at risk. Some of these providers have made plans to work in nearby Illinois, where abortion is still legal and clinics have been overwhelmed by increased demand. Dr. Allie Linton is an OB-GYN (a physician who specializes in obstetrics and gynecology) based in Milwaukee, Wisconsin. She and several of her colleagues were planning to do this. Linton says that the one-hour drive to Illinois is an opportunity to help her patients and Illinois doctors. "I would prefer to provide it in Wisconsin to my patients that don't have to travel across state lines for health care. But I'm so thankful to be able to still utilize my services and to still help these patients receive the care that they deserve,"[45] says Linton.

Employers Pledge Assistance

Traveling to another state for abortion care can be expensive. Patients often must take time off work and also pay for transportation and hotel costs. Women who cannot afford to pay these travel-related costs are left with few options.

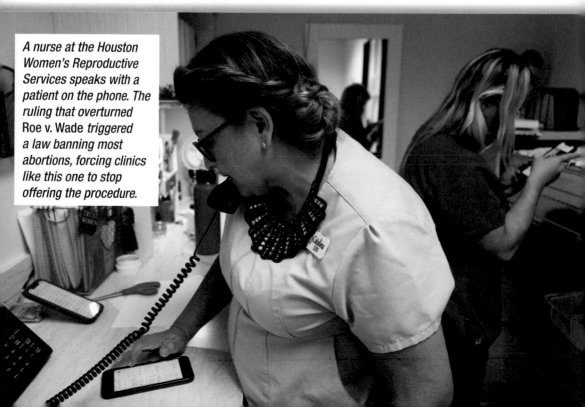

A nurse at the Houston Women's Reproductive Services speaks with a patient on the phone. The ruling that overturned *Roe v. Wade triggered a law banning most abortions, forcing clinics like this one to stop offering the procedure.*

Crisis Pregnancy Centers

Nationwide, crisis pregnancy centers aim to support pregnant women and convince them there are alternatives to abortion. Those alternatives include adoption, counseling and education, and support for pregnancy and parental needs. The centers are frequently religion based and offer services such as pregnancy tests, counseling, and resources such as diapers and baby clothes. One organization, Heartbeat International, has more than twenty-eight hundred locations on six continents. Some of its clinics offer limited ultrasounds, prenatal care, and testing for sexually transmitted diseases. Others offer financial aid classes and mentorship for expecting couples. "Every woman deserves love and support during an unexpected pregnancy. No matter where a woman is in her pregnancy journey, the pregnancy help network provides essential care and support—often at no cost—and will continue to do so because it is the right thing to do," says Andrea Trudden, Heartbeat's vice president of communications and marketing.

Quoted in Heartbeat International, "New Report: Pregnancy Help Organizations Expand Services and Reach, Adapting to New State Laws and Abortion Pathways," May 2, 2021. www.heartbeat international.org.

In response to the Supreme Court ruling, dozens of companies have pledged to cover abortion-related travel costs for their employees. Companies including Amazon, Disney, Apple, and JPMorgan Chase announced they would cover travel costs for any employees who live in states where abortion is illegal and need to travel to terminate a pregnancy. One such company, Patagonia, asserted the company's commitment to covering employees' abortion-related travel expenses. "Caring for employees extends beyond basic health insurance. It means supporting employees' choices around if or when they have a child,"[46] the company stated on social media.

Civitech, a small technology company in Texas, did not wait for the *Dobbs* decision to act. Civitech had committed to covering employee travel expenses for abortions after Texas enacted a law in 2021 that banned abortions after six weeks. The company's chief operating officer, Sarah Jackel, says that employees and investors strongly support the policy. "Employers like us may be the last line of defense," she says. "It makes good business sense. There's no reason we should be putting our employees

Following the overturning of Roe v. Wade, some major corporations, including Apple, pledged to cover the abortion-related expenses of employees who live in states where abortion has been banned and need to travel to states where the procedure is still legal.

in the position of having to choose between keeping their job or carrying out an unwanted pregnancy."[47]

Although numerous companies have pledged to pay for abortion-related travel costs, the specifics of how they will do so remain unclear in many cases. In addition, lawmakers in several states have warned against these types of corporate policies. For example, fourteen state lawmakers in Texas sent a letter to ride-sharing service Lyft warning the company to drop its abortion travel benefit. In news reports, Lyft had no comment. The lawmakers said they plan to introduce legislation to ban companies that pay for abortion care from doing business in Texas.

Abortion Medication

Many women, especially in states that immediately outlawed abortion, have sought other options, including abortion pills (also called medication abortion). Within hours of the *Dobbs* ruling, Just the Pill, a nonprofit organization based in Minnesota that helps patients in several states get abortion pills, received nearly one hundred appointment requests. This was four times the usual number of daily requests.

Before *Dobbs*, abortion pills were already used in nearly half of abortions in the United States. Since *Dobbs*, they have become even more in demand. Abortion pills are approved by the US Food and Drug Administration for use up to the tenth week of pregnancy. The patient takes two different drugs, twenty-four to forty-eight hours apart. The medication halts the development of the pregnancy and then triggers contractions similar to a miscarriage that expel fetal tissue.

Medication abortion is less invasive and more private than a surgical procedure. To order pills, patients fill out an online form or have a consultation with a doctor via video, over the phone, or in person. The pills can be sent by mail and taken privately at home. In 2020, during the COVID-19 pandemic, federal regulators made it easier to get abortion pills by dropping requirements for in-person visits and allowing the medication to be mailed to patients after a virtual appointment. However, patients must obtain the consultation from a doctor in a state where abortion is legal, even if the patients live just over the border.

Self-Managed Abortion

If they cannot get abortion pills from a clinic or doctor, some women are taking matters into their own hands. They are self-managing their abortions, learning about the process online, and finding ways to get the necessary abortion pills. Women who live

Floating Clinic

Dr. Meg Autry, an OB-GYN and founder of the nonprofit PRROWESS (Protecting Reproductive Rights of Women Endangered by State Statutes), has come up with a unique idea to help women access reproductive health care. She is trying to raise $20 million to buy and retrofit a ship that could be used as a floating reproductive health clinic. The floating clinic would be staffed by volunteers and provide low-cost or free surgical abortions up to fourteen weeks of gestation, contraceptives, vaccinations, and testing and treatment for sexually transmitted diseases.

The ship would sail in the Gulf of Mexico, near states that have banned or restricted abortions. It would have to remain outside of those states' territorial waters. That way state laws would not apply, says maritime law expert Matthew Steffey. However, he warns, any of those states could still try to bring legal charges against the ship's patients or providers.

in states where abortion is banned can still get abortion pills on-line from overseas, from international telehealth companies like Aid Access. While US telehealth providers can only provide abortion pills to patients in states where abortion is legal, international doctors face few legal consequences from US state laws. Aid Access's European doctors provide online consultations and prescriptions for abortion pills, filled and mailed from a pharmacy in India. "Under certain circumstances, it will be possible for women to get medication abortion from these internet providers and self manage their abortion, so it will provide some access to some people but not enough,"[48] says Dr. Jennifer Villavicencio of the American College of Obstetricians and Gynecologists.

No one knows how many women are managing their own medication abortions, but experts say more are likely to go this route. Most of the time, medication abortion is safe and has a low risk of complications, even if self-managed by the woman. However, complications can occur, and experts fear that women who encounter problems with self-managed abortions may hesitate to get help in states that have criminalized abortion.

The Battle over Abortion Pills

Medication abortions are by no means a sure thing. States with abortion bans are also targeting this method. Many state laws that ban abortion include language that prohibits all forms of abortion. Nineteen states have prohibited the use of telemedicine for the purpose of obtaining abortion pills. And in Texas a new law even prohibits mail-order abortion pills.

Enforcement of these bans is likely to be much more complicated than shutting down an abortion clinic. Abortion pills can be taken privately at home, and it is impossible to tell the difference between a medication abortion and a miscarriage, since they produce the same symptoms. Additionally, traces of the pills cannot be discovered if taken orally. A woman who needs care after taking abortion pills can claim that she is having a miscarriage. "It's exactly the same symptoms, and the treatment is exactly the same,"[49] says Rebecca Gomperts, a Dutch physician who founded Aid Access,

An employee at a mail-order pharmacy sorts medications. Texas has passed a law to prohibit mail-order abortion medicines.

an organization that screens women online and orders abortion pills from overseas pharmacies that can be mailed to the women.

Abortion rights groups have also stepped in to help women obtain abortion pills. For example, the organization Just the Pill is setting up mobile clinics in states that permit abortion and that border states where the procedure is banned. Patients can cross the border for a consultation and get the pills. The mobile clinic will also provide surgical abortions for those who need them. The clinic plans to open mobile sites in Colorado, New Mexico, and Illinois, since they border states where abortion is already banned or expected to be banned. "By operating on state borders, we will reduce travel burdens for patients in states with bans or severe limits. And by moving beyond a traditional brick-and-mortar clinic, our mobile clinics can quickly adapt to the courts, state legislatures, and the markets, going wherever the need is,"[50] says Dr. Julie Amaon, the organization's medical director.

The *Dobbs* ruling changed the landscape for abortion services in states across the country. As access becomes increasingly restricted in some states, women and providers are turning to alternative methods for abortion care.

CHAPTER SIX

The Push for New National and Interstate Laws

The 2022 *Dobbs* ruling is unlikely to be the final chapter on abortion rights in the United States. Already, both sides are moving to put new laws in place either to further restrict or to protect abortion rights. "We are just beginning to see the ripple effects of the U.S. Supreme Court's decision in *Dobbs vs. Jackson Women's Health Organization*, which eliminated a federal right to choose abortion. So far this much is clear: *Dobbs* will deepen our national divide on abortion for years to come,"[51] says Mary Ziegler, a professor at the University of California, Davis, School of Law.

A National Abortion Ban

Currently, there is no federal law explicitly dealing with abortion rights. Encouraged by the *Dobbs* ruling and state abortion bans, some antiabortion supporters are pushing for a national abortion ban. Former vice president Mike Pence celebrated the overturning of the constitutional right to abortion by calling on all states to enact bans. He said:

> Now that *Roe v. Wade* has been consigned to the ash heap of history, a new arena in the cause of life has emerged, and it is incumbent on all who cherish the sanctity of life to resolve that we will take the defense of the unborn and the support for women in crisis preg-

nancy centers to every state in America. Having been given this second chance for life, we must not rest and must not relent until the sanctity of life is restored to the center of American law in every state in the land.[52]

Some antiabortion lawmakers are pushing for more than statewide bans. At a conference in June 2022, several dozen state legislators from different states brainstormed ideas that would eliminate abortion nationwide. Ideas discussed included a federal law banning the procedure, ways to block access to abortion pills, and limiting the ability to cross state lines for an abortion. "It's not over," says Oklahoma state representative Todd Russ, who attended the conference. "There are all kinds [of ideas] going around."[53]

For any bill to become federal law, it must be passed by the House of Representatives and the Senate and signed into law by the president. Some conservative members of Congress have talked about national legislation prohibiting abortion at fifteen weeks' gestation. In mid-September 2022, one such bill was proposed. Senator Lindsey Graham of South Carolina introduced legislation that would establish a federal ban on abortions after fifteen weeks of pregnancy.

Some members of Congress want to see federal legislation go even further. Representative Mike Kelly from Pennsylvania supports the Heartbeat Protection Act, which would require doctors to check for a fetal heartbeat. An abortion could not be performed once a heartbeat is detected. Typically, this is around six weeks of gestation. And Representative Alex Mooney of West Virginia has proposed the Life at Conception Act, which declares that the constitutional right to life begins at the moment of fertilization. The leaders of several antiabortion groups have called on Congress to call for votes on these and other similar bills. "Only federal law

> "Having been given this second chance for life, we must not rest and must not relent until the sanctity of life is restored to the center of American law in every state in the land."[52]
>
> —Mike Pence, former US vice president

Following the overturning of Roe v. Wade, *Senator Lindsey Graham of South Carolina (at podium) proposed a federal ban on abortions after fifteen weeks of pregnancy.*

can protect unborn babies from states that will continue to allow and even subsidize abortion on demand up until birth. The House of Representatives is best positioned to lead with a robust pro-life agenda,"[54] they wrote.

Legislation to Protect Abortion Rights

At the same time, abortion rights supporters are calling on Congress to pass legislation that guarantees the right to an abortion in all states. In July 2022, after the Supreme Court had overturned *Roe v. Wade*, the House of Representatives passed two bills to protect abortion rights. One is an updated version of the Women's Health Protection Act, which was originally proposed in 2013 and would write abortion rights protections into federal law. The other bill, the Ensuring Access to Abortion Act, would ban states from punishing people who travel to another state for reproductive health care, including abortion. Both bills passed, with mostly Democrats supporting the legislation and mostly Republicans opposing the bills. In a press conference, House Speaker Nancy Pelosi stated that a woman's health decisions "don't belong to politicians in Washington, D.C. or in state capitols or in the

Supreme Court of the United States. They belong to a woman, her family, her God, her doctor, her loved ones."[55]

Also, in July 2022 President Joe Biden signed an executive order to safeguard access to reproductive health care, including abortion and contraception. The order aims to protect patient privacy and promote the safety of patients, providers, and clinics. The administration also issued guidance that the 1985 Emergency Medical Treatment and Active Labor Act permits women to have abortions in an emergency, even in states where the procedure is banned. "Under the law, no matter where you live, women have the right to emergency care—including abortion care. Today, in no uncertain terms, we are reinforcing that we expect providers to continue offering these services and that federal law preempts state abortion bans when needed for emergency care,"[56] says Health and Human Services secretary Xavier Becerra.

Prohibiting Care Across State Lines

It is not uncommon for people to cross state lines—or even US borders—to obtain medical care. Efforts are under way to prohibit this when the medical care being sought is an abortion. Currently, women living in states with abortion restrictions and bans can travel to another state where the procedure is legal if they have the means to do so. In response, some state lawmakers are discussing ways to regulate abortions performed outside of their borders.

Kansas Preserves Abortion Rights

In August 2022 Kansas voters spoke loudly on abortion. Lawmakers in the usually conservative state had proposed removing the right to abortion from the state constitution, but voters resoundingly defeated the ballot referendum. The margin of defeat (with 59 percent voting against the measure and 41 percent supporting it) was surprising to many and encouraging for abortion rights supporters. "The voters in Kansas have spoken loud and clear: We will not tolerate extreme bans on abortion," says Rachel Sweet, the campaign manager for Kansans for Constitutional Freedom, which led the effort to defeat the amendment. Keeping the right to abortion in the state constitution also prevents lawmakers from passing new, restrictive abortion laws. The Kansas ballot referendum is the first of several in US states that will ask voters to decide on abortion rights.

Quoted in Mitch Smith and Katie Glueck, "Kansas Votes to Preserve Abortion Rights Protections in Its Constitution," *New York Times*, August 2, 2022. www.nytimes.com.

In Missouri antiabortion lawmakers have already proposed legislation restricting Missouri residents from getting abortions outside the state. One bill permits private citizens to sue anyone who helps a Missouri resident obtain an abortion in another state. Another bill would apply Missouri's abortion laws to Missouri residents who have an abortion in another state or whose fetus was conceived within the state. Says Rachel Rebouché, an expert in reproductive law:

> The endgame for Missouri is not just to ban abortion in Missouri. The people writing these bills want to ban abortion everywhere. But there are going to be places like California that continue to offer abortion and try to proactively protect their providers and patients. And so the idea of these laws is to try to reach into those states and shield travel to states in which abortion will remain legal.[57]

As of September 2022, neither bill had passed the Missouri state legislature.

Legal experts believe that state efforts to restrict out-of-state abortions are unconstitutional. "We can't reach into another state and penalize people for behavior in that state. One of our foundational understandings is that a state's power stops at their boundaries. And so this idea of extraterritorial jurisdiction, I really do not think is supported by the structure of our Constitution,"[58] says Jessica Levinson, a law professor at Loyola Law School.

Protecting Ability to Seek Care in Other States

States where abortion remains legal are taking measures of their own to block such interference. The governors of Colorado and North Carolina have issued executive orders that protect abortion providers and patients from being extradited to states that prohibit abortion. "This order will help protect North Carolina doctors and nurses and their patients from cruel right-wing criminal laws passed by other states,"[59] North Carolina governor Roy Cooper said in July 2022. In Rhode Island and Maine, the governors signed executive orders stating their states will not cooperate with another state's investigation into abortion patients or providers. States such as New York, California, and Connecticut have also passed or are considering bills to protect abortion providers and patients from extradition, investigation, and civil lawsuits from antiabortion states.

The US Department of Justice has also spoken out against laws that attempt to reach beyond a state's borders. Attorney General Merrick Garland reaffirmed that despite the Supreme

Beyond Abortion

The Supreme Court's reversal of *Roe v. Wade* is based on the reasoning that *Roe* was wrong from the start and that the right to an abortion is not included in the text of the Constitution, nor is it protected as a traditionally recognized constitutional right. Under this reasoning, some court watchers warn that other Supreme Court decisions may be reversed. For example, in *Griswold v. Connecticut* (1965), the court decided that the right to purchase and use contraception was protected by the Constitution. However, that right is not explicitly written in the Constitution, considered when the document was written, or traditionally protected in the country's history. Therefore, some legal scholars expect states to move beyond abortion and pass laws to ban and restrict certain types of contraceptives that work after fertilization, including the morning-after pill and the IUD. Based on this rationale, other non-enumerated rights could also be challenged. One mentioned often is the right to same-sex marriage, established in the 2015 Supreme Court ruling in *Obergefell v. Hodges*.

A doctor speaks with her patient. US Attorney General Merrick Garland has said that states still have the authority to keep abortion legal, and that patients cannot be prohibited from traveling to other states to obtain abortions.

Court's decision to overturn *Roe*, states still had the authority to keep abortion legal. Garland was also clear that states could not restrict crossing state lines for medical treatment under the Constitution. "We recognize that traveling to obtain reproductive care may not be feasible in many circumstances. But under bedrock constitutional principles, women who reside in states that have banned access to comprehensive reproductive care must remain free to seek that care in states where it is legal,"[60] says Garland.

The Supreme Court's decision in *Dobbs v. Jackson Women's Health Organization* and its reversal of *Roe v. Wade* are unlikely to mark the end of the abortion debate. Instead, the *Dobbs* ruling has prompted activists on both sides of the abortion issue to draw new battle lines. The result may be an increase in state versus state cases in the courts, as each side attempts to advance its position and policies.

> "Under bedrock constitutional principles, women who reside in states that have banned access to comprehensive reproductive care must remain free to seek that care in states where it is legal."[60]
>
> —Merrick Garland, US attorney general

SOURCE NOTES

Introduction: The Ruling That Shook a Nation

1. Quoted in Maura Barrett et al., "Rage, Despair, Tears Fill Streets Across Nation as Thousands Protest *Roe* Reversal," NBC News, June 24, 2022. www.nbcnews.com.
2. Quoted in Barrett et al., " Rage, Despair, Tears Fill Streets Across Nation as Thousands Protest *Roe* Reversal."
3. Quoted in US Department of Justice, "Attorney General Merrick B. Garland Statement on Supreme Court Ruling in *Dobbs v. Jackson Women's Health Organization*," June 24, 2022. www.justice.gov.
4. Quoted in Barrett et al., " Rage, Despair, Tears Fill Streets Across Nation as Thousands Protest *Roe* Reversal."
5. Quoted in Elizabeth Dias, "'A Grievous Wrong Was Righted': Anti-Abortion Activists Celebrate the End of *Roe*," *New York Times*, June 24, 2022. www.nytimes.com.
6. Erwin Chemerinsky, "The Enormous Consequences of Overruling *Roe v. Wade*," *Time*, May 3, 2022. https://time.com.

Chapter One: The History of Abortion Rights

7. Quoted in Erin Blakemore, "How U.S. Abortion Laws Went from Nonexistent to Acrimonious," National Geographic, May 17, 2022. www.nationalgeographic.com.
8. Quoted in Blakemore, "How U.S. Abortion Laws Went from Nonexistent to Acrimonious."
9. Quoted in Ashley Welch, "The History of Abortion Rights in the U.S.," Healthline, May 13, 2022. www.healthline.com.
10. Quoted in Welch, "The History of Abortion Rights in the U.S."
11. Quoted in Welch, "The History of Abortion Rights in the U.S."
12. Quoted in Timothy Williams and Alan Blinder, "As States Race to Limit Abortions, Alabama Goes Further, Seeking to Outlaw Most of Them," *New York Times*, May 8, 2019. www.nytimes.com.

Chapter Two: The Ruling That Overturned *Roe*

13. Quoted in Richard Fausset, "Mississippi Bans Abortions After 15 Weeks; Opponents Swiftly Sue," *New York Times*, March 19, 2018. www.nytimes.com.
14. Quoted in Nina Totenberg, "Supreme Court Considers Whether to Reverse *Roe v. Wade*," NPR, December 1, 2021. www.npr.org.
15. Quoted in Center for Reproductive Rights, "*Dobbs v. Jackson Women's Health Organization*: The Case in Depth," March 19, 2018. https://reproductiverights.org.

16. Quoted in Greg Stohr, "Supreme Court Justices Suggest Sweeping Pull-back on Abortion," Bloomberg Law, December 1, 2021. https://news .bloomberglaw.com.
17. Quoted in Center for Reproductive Rights, "At Supreme Court, Center At-torney Defends Precedent, *Roe*, the Right to Liberty, and More," Decem-ber 2, 2021. https://reproductiverights.org.
18. Quoted in National Constitution Center, "*Dobbs v. Jackson Women's Health Organization* (2022)," 2022. https://constitutioncenter.org.
19. Quoted in Saralyn Cruickshank, "Inside the *Dobbs* Decision," Johns Hop-kins University, July 1, 2022. https://hub.jhu.edu.
20. Quoted in Kelsey Reichmann, "Dissent in *Dobbs* Offers a Eulogy for *Roe* and the Rule of Law," Courthouse News Service, June 28, 2022. www .courthousenews.com.
21. Quoted in Reichmann, "Dissent in *Dobbs* Offers a Eulogy for *Roe* and the Rule of Law."
22. Quoted in Reichmann, "Dissent in *Dobbs* Offers a Eulogy for *Roe* and the Rule of Law."
23. Quoted in Reichmann, "Dissent in *Dobbs* Offers a Eulogy for *Roe* and the Rule of Law."

Chapter Three: The States React

24. Quoted in KMBC News, "With Supreme Court Ruling Friday, Missouri 'Trig-ger Law' on Abortion Now in Place," June 24, 2022. www.kmbc.com.
25. Quoted in Dana Branham and Chris Casteel, "End of *Roe* Makes Abortion a Crime in Oklahoma as State's Abortion 'Trigger' Law Takes Effect," *The Oklahoman* (Oklahoma City, OK), June 24, 2022. www.oklahoman.com.
26. Quoted in Eliza Fawcett, "Georgia's 6-Week Abortion Ban Begins Imme-diately After Court Ruling," *New York Times*, July 20, 2022. www.nytimes .com.
27. Quoted in Wynne Davis, "Large Employers Express Opposition After Indi-ana Approves Abortion Ban," NPR, August 6, 2022. www.npr.org.
28. Quoted in Aaron Katersky and Meredith Deliso, "How 3 States Are Moving to Protect Abortion Rights After the Fall of *Roe v. Wade*," ABC News, July 2, 2022. https://abcnews.go.com.
29. Quoted in Katersky and Deliso, "How 3 States Are Moving to Protect Abor-tion Rights After the Fall of *Roe v. Wade*."
30. Quoted in Emma Gallegos, "Gov. Newsom Champions California as a Sanctuary for Those Seeking Abortion," EdSource, June 24, 2022. https:// edsource.org.
31. Quoted in Kyle Cooke, "Gov. Polis Signs Bill Guaranteeing Abortion Access in Colorado," Rocky Mountain PBS, April 4, 2022. www.rmpbs.org.

Chapter Four: Feeling the Effects

32. Quoted in Meghan Holohan and Danielle Campoamor, "Her Pregnancy Won't Survive, and She Can't Get an Abortion: A Heartbroken Mom Speaks Out," MSN, July 11, 2022. www.msn.com.

33. Quoted in Holohan and Campoamor, "Her Pregnancy Won't Survive, and She Can't Get an Abortion."
34. Quoted in Margot Sanger-Katz et al., "Who Gets Abortions in America?," *New York Times*, December 14, 2021. www.nytimes.com.
35. Quoted in Christina Zdanowicz, "Women Have Abortions for Many Reasons Aside from Rape and Incest. Here Are Some of Them," CNN, May 22, 2019. www.cnn.com.
36. Quoted in Michelle Moulton, "Our Abortion Stories: 'If He Had Found Out I Was Pregnant, He Would Have Kidnapped Me and the Baby,'" *Ms.*, July 29, 2022. https://msmagazine.com.
37. Quoted in Alexandria Carolan and Alice Tracey, "'This Is Not About Protecting Life': Supreme Court Overturn of *Roe v. Wade* Threatens Lives of Cancer Patients, Doctors," *Cancer Letter*, July 1, 2022. https://cancer letter.com.
38. Quoted in Ray Sanchez and Melissa Alonso, "Louisiana Woman Who Alleges She Was Denied Abortion After Fetus' Fatal Diagnosis Says 'It Should Not Happen to Any Other Woman,'" CNN, August 26, 2022. www .cnn.com.
39. Quoted in Sanchez and Alonso, "Louisiana Woman Who Alleges She Was Denied Abortion After Fetus' Fatal Diagnosis Says 'It Should Not Happen to Any Other Woman.'"
40. Quoted in Pam Belluck, "They Had Miscarriages, and New Abortion Laws Obstructed Treatment," *New York Times*, July 17, 2022. www.nytimes .com.
41. Quoted in Belluck, "They Had Miscarriages, and New Abortion Laws Obstructed Treatment."

Chapter Five: The Scramble for Abortion Alternatives

42. Ben Cardin, "Cardin Says History Will Show *Dobbs* Decision as 'One of the Worst Decisions of the Supreme Court,'" US Senator Ben Cardin, June 24, 2022. www.cardin.senate.gov.
43. Quoted in Caroline Kitchener, "'We're Done': Chaos and Tears as an Abortion Clinic Abruptly Shuts Down," *Washington Post*, June 24, 2022. www .washingtonpost.com.
44. Quoted in Stephen Paulsen, "Need Care, Will Travel: Abortion Ban Forces Texans Across State Lines," Courthouse News Service, July 1, 2022. www.courthousenews.com.
45. Quoted in Abigail Tracey, "'It's Been a Devastating Several Weeks': Wisconsin Doctors Cross State Lines to Navigate Post-*Roe* Abortion Ban," *Vanity Fair*, July 18, 2022. www.vanityfair.com.
46. Quoted in Emma Goldberg, "These Companies Will Cover Travel Expenses for Employee Abortions," *New York Times*, August 19, 2022. www .nytimes.com.
47. Quoted in Goldberg, "These Companies Will Cover Travel Expenses for Employee Abortions."
48. Quoted in Spencer Kimball, "Women in States That Ban Abortion Will Still Be Able to Get Abortion Pills Online from Overseas," CNBC, June 27, 2022. www.cnbc.com.

49. Quoted in Roni Caryn Rabin, "Some Women 'Self-Manage' Abortions as Access Recedes," *New York Times*, August 7, 2022. www.nytimes.com.
50. Quoted in Pam Belluck, "Abortion Pills Take the Spotlight as States Impose Abortion Bans," *New York Times*, June 26, 2022. www.nytimes.com.

Chapter Six: The Push for New National and Interstate Laws

51. Mary Ziegler, "Op-Ed: *Roe's* Gone, but the Abortion Wars Just Keep Escalating," *Los Angeles Times*, July 30, 2022. www.latimes.com.
52. Quoted in Mariana Alfaro et al., "Pence Calls for National Abortion Ban as Trump, GOP Celebrate End of *Roe*," *Washington Post*, June 24, 2022. www.washingtonpost.com.
53. Quoted in Caroline Kitchener, "*Roe's* Gone. Now Antiabortion Lawmakers Want More," *Washington Post*, June 25, 2022. www.washingtonpost.com.
54. Quoted in Emily Brooks, "House Republicans Weigh National Abortion Restrictions," *The Hill* (Washington, DC), July 7, 2022. https://thehill.com.
55. Quoted in Rebecca Shabad, "House Passes Bills to Protect Abortion Rights; Senate GOP to Block the Legislation," CNBC, July 15, 2022. www.cnbc.com.
56. Quoted in Lauren Egan, "Biden Administration Says Hospitals Must Provide Abortions in Emergencies," NBC News, July 11, 2022. www.nbcnews.com.
57. Quoted in Kaia Hubbard, "Missouri Is Eyeing a Ban on Abortion Beyond Its Borders. It's Happened Before," *U.S. News & World Report*, March 24, 2022. www.usnews.com.
58. Quoted in Hubbard, "Missouri Is Eyeing a Ban on Abortion Beyond Its Borders."
59. Quoted in Jennifer McDermott et al., "States Move to Protect Abortion from Prosecutions Elsewhere," ABC News, July 6, 2022. https://abcnews.go.com.
60. Quoted in US Department of Justice, "Attorney General Merrick B. Garland Statement on Supreme Court Ruling in *Dobbs v. Jackson Women's Health Organization*."

ORGANIZATIONS TO CONTACT

Center for Reproductive Rights
https://reproductiverights.org
The Center for Reproductive Rights is a global legal advocacy organization whose mission is to advance reproductive rights. Its website has information, news, and resources about abortion, contraception, maternal health, and other reproductive health topics.

Centers for Disease Control and Prevention (CDC)
www.cdc.gov
The CDC is the premier public health agency in the United States. Its website includes the latest information about abortion, pregnancy, and reproductive health.

Guttmacher Institute
www.guttmacher.org
The Guttmacher Institute is a leading research and policy organization focusing on sexual and reproductive health and rights in the United States and worldwide. Its website features information, research, and news about abortion, contraception, and other reproductive health issues.

National Constitution Center
https://constitutioncenter.org
The National Constitution Center is the leading platform for constitutional education. Its website provides the full text of the Constitution and its amendments, as well as a library of Supreme Court cases.

National Right to Life Committee
www.nrlc.org
The National Right to Life Committee is the country's largest pro-life organization, with more than three thousand local chapters nationwide. Its website features fact sheets and information about various abortion issues and related state and federal legislation.

Students for Life of America
https://studentsforlife.org
Students for Life of America is a nonprofit antiabortion organization for high school and college students. Its website offers information for students, including a section with facts about abortion, abortion alternatives, human development, birth control, and more.

FOR FURTHER RESEARCH

Books

Meghan Green, *Abortion: A Continuing Debate*. New York: Lucent, 2018.

New York Times editorial staff, *Abortion: Changing Perspectives.* New York: Rosen, 2019.

Leslie J. Reagan, *When Abortion Was a Crime: Women, Medicine, and Law in the United States, 1867–1973*. Oakland: University of California Press, 2022.

Robin Stevenson, *My Body, My Choice: The Fight for Abortion Rights*. Victoria, British Columbia: Orca, 2019.

Christine Wilcox, *Thinking Critically: Abortion*. San Diego: ReferencePoint, 2018.

Internet Sources

New York Times, "The *Dobbs v. Jackson* Decision, Annotated," June 24, 2022. www.nytimes.com.

New York Times, "Tracking the States Where Abortion Is Now Banned," August 26, 2022. www.nytimes.com.

NPR, "Supreme Court Overturns *Roe v. Wade*, Ending Right to Abortion Upheld for Decades," June 24, 2022. www.npr.org.

Pew Research Center, "Majority of Public Disapproves of Supreme Court's Decision to Overturn *Roe v. Wade*," July 6, 2022. www.pewresearch.org.

Saima May Sidik, "The Effects of Overturning *Roe v. Wade* in Seven Simple Charts," *Nature*, August 10, 2022. www.nature.com.

INDEX